To Newcastle Lions -
Happy reading!

Jim White
(EDITOR)

3/20/18

THE HISPANIC INFLUENCE IN THE UNITED STATES

LATINOS
IN AMERICAN HISTORY

ALVAR NUNEZ CABEZA
DE VACA

BY VALERIE MENARD

Newcastle Elementary School
8400 136th Ave. SE
Newcastle, WA 98059
425-837-5825

Mitchell Lane
PUBLISHERS

P.O. Box 196
Hockessin, Delaware 19707

THE HISPANIC INFLUENCE IN THE UNITED STATES

LATINOS
IN AMERICAN HISTORY

OTHER TITLES IN THE SERIES

Alvar Nuñez Cabeza de Vaca

Hernando de Soto

Juan Ponce de Leon

Pedro Menendez de Aviles

Gaspar de Portola

Mariano Guadalupe Vallejo

Francisco Vasquez de Coronado

Lorenzo de Zavala

Dolores Huerta

Jovita Idar

Octaviano Larrazolo

Fray Juan Crespi

Americo Paredes

Juan Bautista de Anza

Diego Rivera

Juan Rodriguez Cabrillo

Junipero Jose Serra

Bernardo de Galvez

Cesar Chavez

Antonio Lopez de Santa Anna

Visit us on the web: www.mitchelllane.com
Comments? email us: mitchelllane@mitchelllane.com

THE HISPANIC INFLUENCE IN THE UNITED STATES

LATINOS
IN AMERICAN HISTORY

ALVAR NUNEZ CABEZA
DE VACA

BY VALERIE MENARD

Mitchell Lane
PUBLISHERS

Printing   2   3   4   5   6   7   8   9

Library of Congress Cataloging-in-Publication Data

Menard, Valerie.
     Alvar Nunez Cabeza de Vaca / Valerie Menard.
         p. cm. -- (Latinos in American history)
Summary: Discusses the life and exploration of a descendant of Spanish politicians, Alvar
   Nunez Cabeza de Vaca, who came to America as a conquistador but was captured and
   made a slave.
Includes bibliographical references and index.
     ISBN 1-58415-153-6 (lib. bdg.)
     1. Nâuänez Cabeza de Vaca, Alvar, 16th cent.--Juvenile literature. 2. Explorers--America-
   -Biography--Juvenile literature. 3. Explorers--Spain--Biography--Juvenile literature. 4.
   America--Discovery and exploration--Spanish--Juvenile literature. [1. Cabeza de Vaca,
   Alvar Nâuänez, 16th cent. 2. Explorers. 3. America--Discovery and exploration--Spanish.]
   I. Title. II. Series.
     E125.N9 M46 2002
     970.01'6'092--dc21   2002008331

ABOUT THE AUTHOR: Valerie Menard is a freelance writer. She was hired as an editor for Hispanic magazine when the magazine moved from Washington, D.C. to Austin, Texas, in July 1994 and remained with the magazine through 1999, when it relocated to Miami, Florida. Before joining the magazine, she was the managing editor for five years of an Austin bilingual weekly, *La Prensa*. At *La Prensa*, Valerie became an expert on the Hispanic market and an advocate for Latino causes. At *Hispanic*, she promoted stories that addressed the important political and social issues facing Latinos. As a freelance writer she has written for several publications including: *The Austin American Statesman, Estylo, Latina Style, Red Herring, Hispanic,* and *Vista.* She has also written biographical books for children as part of the *Real-Life Reader Biography* series and in 2000, her first solo book project, *The Latino Holiday Book*, was published by Marlowe and Company. The book is in its fifth printing and the Spanish version will be published in 2002 by Random House Español.

PHOTO CREDITS: Cover: Hulton/Archive; p. 6 Archivo Iconografico, S.A./Corbis; p. 10 Ted Spiegel/Corbis; p. 12 North Wind Picture Archives; p. 14 Bettmann/Corbis; p. 16 Stephanie Kondrchek; p. 18 Bettmann/Corbis; p. 24 North Wind Picture Archives; p. 30 Hulton/Archive; p. 34 SuperStock; p. 36 Corbis

PUBLISHER'S NOTE: This story is based on the author's extensive research, which she believes to be accurate. Some parts of the text might have been created by the author based on her research to illustrate what might have happened years ago, and is solely an aid to readability for young adults.

    The spelling of the names in this book follow the generally accepted usage of modern day. The spelling of Spanish names in English has evolved over time with no consistency. Many names have been anglicized and no longer use the accent marks or any Spanish grammar. Others have retained the Spanish grammar. Hence, we refer to Hernando de Soto as "de Soto," but Francisco Vásquez de Coronado as "Coronado." There are other variances as well. Some sources might spell Vásquez as Vazquez. For the most part, we have adapted the more widely recognized spellings.

CONTENTS

CHAPTER 1

The battle between the Christians and Moors for control of Spain ended in 1492 with the fall of Granada, the last city in Spain controlled by the Moors.

BORN INTO A VIOLENT WORLD

The world of the late 15th and early 16th centuries would seem incredible to anyone from the 21st. It was a period in history marked by violence from wars and conquests. There were several world powers at the time—England, France and Spain among them—and they were all vying for the number-one position. They had to fight off invasions, disease, and internal uprisings as well as try to conquer other nations and acquire more wealth to increase their power.

This was a bloody period in history but it was also extremely significant. It is called the Renaissance, a French word that means "rebirth." It lasted for about 300 years between the 14th and 17th centuries. It's called the rebirth because it followed the Medieval Era, a much darker time in Europe when cities were walled in to protect against invasion and disease. The Renaissance shed many superstitions and fears, and replaced them with more inquisitive efforts. It was a great period of evolution and discovery in the arts and sciences.

It was also a great period of exploration and discovery of new worlds, especially by the Spanish. They were the new kids on the block among world powers because they had just freed themselves from domination by the Islamic Moors after a seven-century struggle known as the *Reconquista*, or Reconquest. The Moors crossed over to

Spain from North Africa early in the eighth century and quickly took control of the entire country.

The Spanish fought back, and slowly began to reclaim their territory. The Moors were finally driven out of their last foothold in Spain early in 1492. Christopher Columbus sailed later that year and discovered the New World. Within a few decades, Spanish explorers and colonists had established themselves in Mexico, Central America and South America. They sent vast amounts of treasure that included gold and silver back to Spain. That wealth quickly made the Spanish a major power in Europe.

Still, the Spanish were more conservative than their fellow Europeans. Religion inspired the Spaniards as much as the arts or sciences. They embraced the Catholic faith with extreme enthusiasm. Morris Bishop described the Spanish character of the Renaissance in his book *The Odyssey of Cabeza de Vaca*: "The Spaniard was merciless to infidel and heretic...inhabited more by the fires of passion than his neighbors to the foggy north (England), he (the Spaniard) was extreme, fanatical, and wholly unsympathetic with his opponents and their beliefs and feelings."

These beliefs not only spurred the Spaniards to explore new worlds, they also assisted them in their ruthless destruction of the natives whom they discovered when they landed.

Álvar Núñez Cabeza de Vaca (AL-var NOON-yehz kah-BAY-zuh duh VAHK-uh) was born during this violent era in the year 1490. His birthplace was Jerez de la Frontera, a city in southwestern Spain just a few miles inland from the port city of Cadíz.

Álvar's parents were Francisco de Vera and Doña Teresa Cabeza de Vaca. His father was a respected man and held political office in Jerez. De Vera's father, Pedro de Vera Mendoza was much more notorious.

He was fiercely loyal to Spain's King Henry IV and was called upon by his majesty to perform several brutal acts. One time he heard a man plotting against the king. So he challenged the man to a duel and killed him. Then he cut out the man's tongue and gave it to the king as proof of his loyalty.

He became famous for the conquest of Grand Canary Island for Spain in 1480. It was one of the Canary Islands that are located off the coast of Northern Africa. After he finished subduing the Guanches, the native inhabitants of the island, he invited them to join him and his soldiers in an invasion of a neighboring island. He even swore an oath that he would reward them. Hundreds swarmed onto his ship. But he sold them into slavery instead.

Cabeza de Vaca was about ten years old when his grandfather died, but Morris Bishop supposes that he must have developed an early interest in foreign lands by listening to his grandfather's tales.

"In the interval between his retirement and his death he had for an auditor (listener) the boy Álvar Núñez Cabeza de Vaca, the eldest child of his son Francisco," Bishop wrote. "Telling his fond stories, he recognized in the boy's ardor an early sympathy of spirit, while little Álvar Núñez learned from his fierce old grandfather the honor of courage and fortitude and the scorn of death."

From a young age, Álvar may have wanted to match the great deeds of his grandfather. Certainly he was exposed to native peoples through his grandfather, who brought back many Guanches to work as slaves. They sang to the boy in their own language and told him stories about their former home. Bishop wrote: "They gave him a sense of familiarity with inarticulate brown men...this would be lost with his later education, and was to be recovered only when, on the barbarous coasts of the New World, the brown men were his masters and he the slave."

His mother's side of the family was just as important. They were the ones from whom the name Cabeza de Vaca stemmed. It means literally "head of a cow" and there is a legend about its origin.

It begins in the 13th century during the *Reconquista*. Following one battle in 1212, the Moors were forced to retreat southward into the Sierra Morena Mountains, where the rough landscape allowed them to regroup and fortify themselves. They controlled the passes through the mountains. The Christian soldiers knew that they would be picked off or ambushed if they tried to follow the Moors into the mountains.

They prepared to retreat but a shepherd named Martín Alhaja came forward with a plan. He knew of a pass that was not protected by the Moors where the Christians could enter and trap them. He marked the spot with a cow's skull. The plan worked and the Christians successfully defeated the Moors in what became known as the Battle of Las Novas de Tolosa. It was one of the most decisive battles of the *Reconquista*.

King Sancho de Navarre rewarded Alhaja by establishing him and his descendants as members of nobility and changing their name from Alhaja to Cabeza de Vaca.

It may seem strange that Álvar used his mother's last name rather than his father's but this was often the custom in Spain at the time. His siblings used their father's last name as their middle and their mother's last name as their last, such as his brother Juan de Vera Cabeza de Vaca.

With a family that included soldiers as well as nobles, it seems natural that Álvar would take up a military career. He received his first assignment at the age of 21. It was the spring of 1511 and the French had invaded Italy. The pope at the time, Pope Julius II, asked Spain's King Ferdinand II for support. Álvar was one of the soldiers sent to fight the French. He survived many bloody battles, including the

In 1511, Pope Julius II enlisted the help of Spain in the effort to free Italy from a French invasion.

battle of Ravenna on April 11, 1512 where 20,000 died. For his performance as a soldier, Cabeza de Vaca was promoted to lieutenant and stationed in Gaeta, Italy.

He returned to Spain about a year later and served under the Duke of Medina Sidonia. He was sent to fight again seven years later against the rebels in an uprising in Seville. For his loyalty, he was appointed to command a city gate outside of Seville, the Puerta del Ossario.

At this point, the historical record runs out for several years. He probably married during this time. There is proof that he had a wife because Cabeza de Vaca mentions her in his memoirs. But we don't know her name and there is no evidence that they had any children.

Living in Seville, Cabeza de Vaca must have seen first-hand the results of the voyages to the New World. Located on the Guadalquivir (gwod-el-KWEEV-er or gwod-el-kee-VEER) River that flows directly into the Atlantic Ocean, the city was a major port. Returning ships would tie up on the piers and unload the treasures they'd carried back across the ocean. These exotic sights may well have fired his imagination.

This is the world in which Cabeza de Vaca grew up. It was enlightened in some ways because scholars were beginning to talk about concepts like equality among all human creatures, but at the same time carried remnants of the barbarism of the medieval period. People may have begun to consider the value of their fellow man but non-Christians were still judged to be savages and less than human.

Cabeza de Vaca was probably not much different from the rest of his countrymen. In his mid-thirties, he was a seasoned military officer and no stranger to the brutality of war. Like the conquistadors before him, he was ready to conquer more land for Spain and bring back more riches in gold and silver, regardless of the human sacrifice.

But the tables would turn on Cabeza de Vaca and he would live as a slave, not a conqueror.■

The Narváez Expedition set sail in five caravels, small boats that were shorter than a modern basketball court and filled to the brim with supplies.

ACROSS THE ATLANTIC

Cabeza de Vaca re-enters history in 1527. No one knows what he had done during the previous six years, but it must have been important. He was named treasurer, or second in command, of an expedition to Florida.

This wasn't the first time that the Spanish had tried to take Florida. Inspired by rumors of vast riches, Juan Ponce de León had discovered it in 1513, then returned eight years later in an effort to colonize it. But both times he encountered fierce resistance from the Indians. He was wounded by an arrow in the thigh during the second expedition. It quickly became infected and he died from the wound. Several other Spanish explorers didn't have any more luck. But in spite of these difficulties, the Spanish continued to believe that Florida contained the same vast riches that they had already discovered in other parts of the New World.

This new expedition was under the command of Pánfilo de Narváez. He was probably born sometime between 1470 and 1480 and appears to have arrived in the New World about 1510 or 1511. After helping the Spanish to dominate Jamaica, he served under the command of the governor of Cuba, Diego de Velázquez. Narváez was primarily responsible for conquering the island.

He quickly earned a reputation for cruelty towards the natives. Catholic priests were beginning to defend the natives and to criticize the harsh way the Spaniards treated them. In the case of Narváez, that priest was Bartolomé de las Casas.

De las Casas wrote of one occasion where the Spaniards, after sharing a meal with the inhabitants of a Cuban village, began murdering them without any cause. The priest, who managed to save a few lives, noticed Narváez watching the killing without expression.

"And what does your worship think of what our Spaniards have done?" he asked de las Casas.

One of the few priests to speak out, Father Bartolomé de las Casas disagreed with the mistreatment of the natives and was further appalled when he witnessed the senseless slaughter of one village by Narvaéz.

The priest answered: "I offer them and you too to the devil."

Still, Narváez was simply following orders. According to Bishop: "The hatred of the priest and the natives for Narváez was countered by the approval of his superiors....By 1520 he was back in Cuba enjoying his wealth in land and Indians."

Narváez would also cross paths with the infamous conquistador Hernán Cortés, who had sailed from Cuba and conquered the Aztecs in Mexico in 1519. But he had exceeded the authority that Governor Velázquez had given him. So Velázquez sent Narváez to Mexico with an army of nearly 1,000 men early the following year to arrest Cortés and bring him back to Cuba in chains.

Though he was outnumbered by at least three to one, Cortés was a much better leader than Narváez. He made a daring nighttime attack and defeated the over-confident Narváez, who lost one of his eyes during the battle. Cortés recruited most of Narváez' men to join him and share in the Aztec treasure. Then he threw Narváez into prison for three years.

When he was released, he returned to Spain. Eventually he was named as Ponce de León's replacement as governor of Florida. He also received a charter for all the territory between Florida and what was known as the River of Palms, almost certainly today's Rio Grande River in Texas.

Cabeza de Vaca's appointment as treasurer came in early 1527. He was in charge of all the collected revenue, such as gold and silver, during the expedition. He also had to collect taxes from all the revenue and applicable rent, and pay the officers their salaries.

Complaints from the Catholic missionaries regarding treatment of the natives had impressed the Spanish nobility. So for this voyage, Cabeza de Vaca was also ordered to observe the treatment of the natives and report back.

The Narváez expedition set sail with five ships, or caravels, and about 600 men on June 17, 1527. Even though the trip across the Atlantic was completed without any major problems, it still wasn't easy. The journey required several weeks in vessels that were all shorter than a modern basketball court. They were jam-packed with supplies, so there was very little room for the men to sit down or sleep.

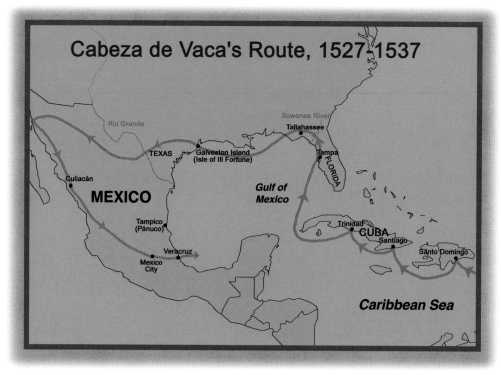

This map shows Cabeza de Vaca's route through America. In 1527 they arrived in Santo Domingo, in the Dominican Republic. It would take them almost a year since setting sail from Spain to land in Florida, which they did in April 1528.

The food quickly turned bad, and it wasn't unusual for the hardtack, or ship's biscuits, to be filled with maggots and cockroaches.

Finally they arrived at the port of Santo Domingo on the island of Española (modern-day Hispaniola, where both Haiti and the Dominican Republic are located). More than 100 of the men had already had enough. So they deserted. Everyone else remained there for 45 days, collecting supplies and horses for the rest of the trip.

They sailed on to Santiago on the southern coast of Cuba. Narváez ordered Cabeza de Vaca to take two ships and travel further up the coast to Trinidad for additional supplies. This is where Cabeza de Vaca's luck began to change.

A hurricane struck while they were anchored there. Cabeza de Vaca and about 30 men were the only survivors since they had gone ashore to help organize the cargo for loading. Both ships, 60 men and 20 horses were lost. The force of the storm was so fierce that one of the ship's lifeboats wound up in a tree more than a mile inland.

Cabeza de Vaca wrote what is the earliest known description of a West Indian hurricane. "Then the rain and the storm increased in violence, and all the houses and churches fell down, and we had to go about seven or eight men locking arms at a time, to prevent the wind from carrying us off...we heard, all night long and especially after midnight, a great uproar, the sound of many voices, the tinkling of little bells, also flutes and tambourines and other instruments, the most of which lasted until morning when the storm ceased. Never has such a fearful thing been witnessed in those parts."

Luckily, Narváez and his ships had survived the storm. They arrived a few days later and rescued Cabeza de Vaca and the others. The men were so frightened by the experience that Narváez decided to wait until spring to go any further. So they spent the winter months recovering and preparing for the expedition to resume.

During that time, Narváez found a pilot named Miruelo who claimed to be familiar with the waters around Florida. The expedition set off again in late February. By the best estimates, it consisted of five ships, 400 men and 80 horses. One ship was left behind with additional supplies.

Little did they suspect that most of them would be dead within a few months.■

Once it landed in North America, the Narváez Expedition faced starvation and Indian attacks as it traveled from Florida to Texas.

DISASTER STRIKES

T he expedition didn't get off to a good start. "The touted (highly regarded) pilot we had taken on ran the vessels aground," Cabeza de Vaca commented sarcastically in *La Relación*, the book he would later write about his experiences. "For fifteen days we stood stranded, the keels often scraping bottom. At last a storm from the south raised the water over the shoals enough to lift us off, though dangerously."

After surviving two more storms, the ships finally sighted the coast of western Florida on April 12, 1528. It had taken them more than 40 days to cover about 500 miles. They sailed just offshore for two more days before dropping anchor, most likely at either Clearwater Bay or Sarasota Bay in the Tampa/St. Petersburg area.

On the following day, which was Good Friday, Narváez and some of the men went ashore. They encountered an Indian village that had been deserted. Narváez claimed the land in the name of Charles I, the Spanish King.

The rest of the men landed and began exploring the territory. Narváez, however, was interested in finding a certain port that Miruelo, his pilot, had described. So he sent one ship up the coast to continue looking for the port. Then the captain was supposed to return to Cuba to get the ship that had been left behind with additional supplies. The delays in arriving in Florida had seriously depleted the amount of food that was available.

Cabeza de Vaca got in a final dig at Miruelo: "He did not know where we were or where the port was from here."

The expedition proceeded inland for several miles. There they discovered a village known as Ucita. They found several small gold ornaments. But Hirrihigua, the village chief, wouldn't say where they had come from. So Narváez hacked off the unfortunate man's nose. At that point, Hirrihigua gestured vaguely to the north and told of the great wealth of a tribe known as the Apalachee. They lived in Apalachen. It was described as a large, important city.

That was all Narváez needed. He proposed to take most of the men in the expedition, about 300 men, and march inland to Apalachen. The rest would remain with the ships, which would sail just offshore. The two groups would meet at a port named Pánuco. The pilot believed that it was nearby, within 100 miles. But he was wrong. At that time, no one realized the immense size of the newly discovered North American continent. Pánuco (modern-day Tampico, Mexico) was 1,800 miles away.

His error would sound the death knell for about 300 men.

Cabeza de Vaca opposed the plan. "I answered, that under no circumstances should we forsake the ships before they rested in a secure harbor which we controlled," he wrote. He added other objections: no one really knew where they were, they had only limited food, they had no one who could speak the Indians' language.

It didn't matter. Only one officer agreed with him. The rest went along with Narváez, who then offered Cabeza de Vaca the option of staying with the ships.

He chose to join the inland expedition. According to Cleve Hallenbeck in his book *Álvar Núñez Cabeza de Vaca*: "Núñez (Cabeza de Vaca) declined, despite the urging of Narváez and others, saying that while he felt sure the expedition never would see the ships again, his honor required that he share the perils of the inland expedition with his comrades."

That expedition began on May 1, 1528. The folly of Narváez' plan quickly became apparent. Much of Florida is swampy. It is filled with poisonous snakes and mosquitos. As the season advances, it also becomes very hot. The men, wearing heavy armor, must have been very uncomfortable.

After a few weeks they crossed the Suwanee River, most of the way up Florida's west coast. After crossing the river they were met by about 200 Indians who looked fairly fierce. The Spaniards immediately began to fight them and captured five or six who led them to their village. They stayed there for a few days, eating, resting, and gathering more food for the journey.

Nearly two months after they started, they came in sight of Apalachen, which was probably near present-day Tallahassee, the state capital of Florida.

"We have many thanks to God to be near this destination, believing everything we had been told about it and expecting an immediate end of our hardships," Cabeza de Vaca wrote.

He couldn't have been more wrong.

The town had only about 40 small thatched huts, a little food, and no gold. It also had lots of angry Indians, who had abandoned the town when the Spaniards approached. They fired arrows from places of concealment. None of the Spaniards were killed but many were injured. After nearly a month in Apalachen, Narváez decided it would be better to retreat.

From captured Indians, they learned of a village known as Aute, further west and south. It had plenty of food, they were told. They arrived there nine days later to find the village abandoned. But the fields were filled with unharvested corn, beans, and squash.

After a few days of rest, Narváez sent Cabeza de Vaca with 50 men to explore the coast to find an entrance to the sea. They found inlets and bays but not the sea itself. When they returned, they found that the expedition had been attacked. Many men were wounded and others were sick. Narváez opted to move further south, if only to get away from more Indian attacks.

By now, the expedition was in serious trouble. In addition to hunger and arrow wounds, the men who were riding horses wanted to leave. They believed that they could travel faster without waiting for the exhausted infantrymen to keep up with them.

In an effort to keep his little army together, Narváez came up with a final solution. He instructed the men to build boats from whatever wood they could find and they would all try to sail to Pánuco. But they knew nothing about building boats. Only one of the men was a carpenter and he didn't even have basic tools such as saws.

However, the men were resourceful.

"They made bellows (pumps) out of deer hide, and of their stirrups, spurs, and crossbows, knives, etc., they made the tools and nails required for the work," wrote Hallenbeck. "The fibers of the palmetto (tree) were used for oakum (caulking), and pitch (resin) was obtained from certain pine trees. The manes and tails of the horses were converted into ropes and the shirts of the men were made into sails."

They began work on August 4, 1528 in a sheltered inlet which they named Bahia de Caballos (Bay of Horses) in honor of the animals that were keeping them alive. Cabeza de Vaca explained that every third day they would kill one of the remaining horses and eat it, then make its skin into bags to carry fresh water during the voyage. They also raided nearby Indian settlements for additional food.

By September 20 they had finished building five barges that were probably no more than 30 feet long. They departed two days later. With nearly 50 men packed tightly into each one, they had less than a foot of freeboard, or the amount of space between the sea and the edge of the boats. Cabeza de Vaca commanded one of the boats, which contained most of the sick men—probably a sign of the dislike that he and Narváez had for each other.

It took a week just to find open water. Then the little flotilla headed west along the coast, still in the belief that Pánuco was not far away. Dependent on wind, current and occasional paddling, they could only make a few miles each day.

In addition to the crowded conditions, there were other problems. They didn't have much food. And they began to run low on fresh water as the bags made of horsehide started to fall apart.

A month later, they were hit by a storm. They were stuck on a small island for six days. According to Hallenbeck, "their thirst became so tormenting that some of the men drank sea water, which resulted in the death of five of them." They also encountered a hostile tribe of Indians who forced them to leave the island and head back into the storm.

They continued on the journey, meeting friendly and hostile Indians along the way. Eventually, they reached the mouth of the Mississippi River. Even several miles out at sea, it provided them with much-needed fresh water. But a strong current began to push the barges even further away from land. The tiny vessels became separated in the night. Cabeza de Vaca sighted two barges the following day. One carried Narváez.

"What do you think we should do?" the governor asked him.

"Join the barge ahead," Cabeza de Vaca replied. "By no means abandon her; so the three might go where God willed, together."

But Narváez was more concerned about saving his own skin. "It is too far out to sea and I want to get to shore," he said. "If you wish to follow me, order your men to the oars. Only by arm work can the land be gained."

Cabeza de Vaca tried to keep up with Narváez. But his men, many of whom were still weakened from the illnesses they had contracted back in Florida, were much more exhausted than the governor's. His barge began to fall behind.

"Throw me a rope so we can stay with you," he shouted.

Narváez refused. "I can't sap my men's strength," he said.

"Then what should I do?" Cabeza de Vaca yelled.

"Every man must do what he thinks best to save himself," his leader replied. Then he pulled away.

It was the last time Cabeza de Vaca would see the expedition's leader.

It was the end of Narváez. It was just the beginning of their problems.■

Cabeza de Vaca proved to be a good leader as he took his men ahead of the Narváez Expedition to find a port named Pánuco.

THE CONQUISTADOR BECOMES A SLAVE

rue to his word, Cabeza de Vaca caught up with the other barge. But another storm came up and sank it. Though his barge managed to survive, the men were so exhausted after a steady diet of half a handful of raw corn each day that they were unable to stand. It was also bitterly cold. Cabeza de Vaca probably assumed that they would soon be dead as well.

He would have been wrong.

Just before dawn on November 6, 1528, he heard the roar of breakers. Soon the boat was cast ashore on what is likely Galveston Island, just off the Texas coast. When they landed, most of the men were already near death. But the warmth from a campfire and the taste of cooked corn seemed to do wonders. They even found some rainwater to ease their thirst.

Cabeza de Vaca sent one of his men to investigate inland and he found an Indian village. On his way back, he met three armed Indians. These Indians were turned away by members of the crew who had gone in search of the first scout. But soon 100 warriors returned to confront the Spaniards.

"They looked like giants to us," Cabeza de Vaca wrote. "We could not hope to defend ourselves; not half a dozen of us could even stand up."

Unlike Narváez, Cabeza de Vaca assumed a diplomatic approach. He offered presents of beads and little bells to the Indians, who gave each Spaniard an arrow as a token of friendship. Cabeza de Vaca made it clear that they were hungry and not a threat. The next morning the Indians returned with fish and edible roots. They came again in the evening with more food and continued to do so for several days.

The men recovered and talked about putting to sea again. Their boat had been washed ashore and was practically buried in the sand. The Spaniards took off their clothes to better perform the task of launching the boat.

But within moments of scrambling back on board and paddling away from the beach, a large wave hit them. A second wave capsized the boat. The barge sank, taking all their clothes with it. Three men were trapped in the sunken hulk and drowned. The rest were washed back on shore. Cold, exhausted, and naked, the men began to weep. The Indians arrived on schedule with another meal but were surprised to find the men naked and distressed.

This was a compassionate tribe. Cabeza de Vaca wrote, "When the Indians saw the disaster we were in, they sat down among us and with great grief and pity they felt on seeing us in such a desperate plight, all of them began to weep loudly, and so sincerely that they could be heard a long way off."

Then he added, "It was amazing to see these wild, untaught savages howling like brutes in compassion for us."

In time he would come to have a very different view of the Indians. In many ways the "savages" would be his own countrymen.

Cabeza de Vaca asked the Indians to take them to their village. A few days later, they discovered more survivors of the expedition including captains Andrés Dorantes and Alonso del Castillo. They had survived with all their men, about 80. They had no clothes to offer Cabeza de Vaca and his men but they did suggest that they try to repair their boat. Once again, they did not have luck on their side and the boat sank.

They were already in the month of November and the weather was getting cold. Cabeza de Vaca knew that the only way to survive was to stay in the village. Some of his men were afraid, sure that they would become the victims of human sacrifice. But that wasn't the case.

They did have one close call. A desperate group of Spaniards who had settled along the beach began to eat each other. When the Indians heard this, they were shocked. They realized that the Spaniards were too barbaric to keep around and decided that all of them should be killed.

Luckily, one Indian spoke up for the Spaniards and convinced the tribe to spare them. Cabeza de Vaca wrote: "And it was Our Lord's will that the others followed his advice and opinion, and thus their plan was thwarted. We gave to this island the name of Malhado, Isle of Ill Fortune."

The weather turned even colder. The food supply dwindled. The Spanish shivered uncontrollably in the huts, which were exposed to the elements.

By the end of winter, the few Spaniards who had survived were by no means conquistadors. They depended on the Indians fully for their survival and recognizing this, the Indians put them to work as slaves. Not all the work was lowly, however. At one point, the Indians wanted to teach them the arts of healing and make them medicine men. The Indians seemed impressed with Cabeza de Vaca's prayers. Although he resisted at first, Cabeza de Vaca soon began to learn about plants and other methods the Indians used for healing.

Cabeza de Vaca was separated from the other Spaniards because he became very ill. It took him a year to recover. But when he regained his health, he was treated very poorly and beaten so badly that he decided to escape. He was successful and for the next few years became a trader of goods among the tribes.

"I was free to go wherever I wished and was not obliged to do anything and was not a slave; and everywhere I went they gave me good treatment and food on account of my merchandise," he wrote.

Although he had an opportunity to explore—some historians believe that he wandered as far north as Oklahoma—and more free-

dom as a trader, Cabeza de Vaca opted to stay close to the Isle of Ill
Fortune. He knew there were some Spaniards still held captive there.
He hoped to find a way to free them. He was especially curious about
Lope de Oviedo, Alonso del Castillo, and Andrés Dorantes. He would
eventually be reunited with these men, as well as the African slave
Estebanico. They were the final remaining survivors of the 300 men
who had gone ashore in Florida several years earlier. But his determi-
nation to keep close to his countrymen forced him back into slavery
with the Indians.

Lope de Oviedo returned to his old tribe and remained a slave but
the other four were re-united and remained together for the next two
years while they plotted how to escape from the Indians who held
them captive. It all depended on the prickly pear season when the
entire village would go out to harvest the cactus fruit and leave the
slaves behind with a few Indians as guards.

After six months, that time came but their chance of escape was
ruined by an argument between the Indians. They had to wait another
year to try again. During this time, Cabeza de Vaca was severely mis-
treated.

When the prickly pear season came again, they successfully escaped. This was probably about September 1534. From then on, they
would be held in high esteem by the Indians they encountered. Their
days of slavery were over.

Repeatedly, they would come upon Indians who had heard of their
healing powers. They would place their hands upon the sick and make
the sign of the cross. The sick men frequently seemed to get better. In
return, the Indians gave them gifts, like food and deerskins.

"And we never healed anyone who did not then tell us that he was
well, and that they were so confident that they would be cured if we
healed them, that they believed that as long as we were there none of
them would have to die," Cabeza de Vaca explained.

The four men continued this way for the rest of their journey.
They traveled from one Indian village to the next, curing the sick and
receiving enough food and supplies to carry them onto the next village.

Sometime the following summer they crossed the Rio Grande
River. It forms the border between modern-day Texas and Mexico.

They were now less than 300 miles from the elusive Pánuco. Mexico City was another 200 miles further. But they received warnings that the Indians they would encounter on that route would kill them on sight as white men.

So they headed north and west through the mountains for what ultimately added 1,500 miles to their journey. When they reached the western coast of Mexico about six months later, the men heard rumors that other Christians—Spaniards—were in the area.

By this time, many Indians were following the four men, as if they were religious prophets. But when they heard that Spaniards were coming, many threatened to leave in fear. Cabeza de Vaca convinced them that no harm would come to them and they stayed.

This was one of the keys to their ability to survive. They had learned to speak the languages of many tribes and to respect their cultures and beliefs. In turn, the Indians had provided food and helped guide them to other villages. Without their help, Cabeza de Vaca and his men could have wandered into the desert where they would certainly have died.

They sent messengers on ahead to find the Spaniards.

"And next morning I overtook four mounted Christians, who were thunderstruck to see me so strangely dressed and in the company of Indians," Cabeza de Vaca wrote. He asked them to take him to their leader, Diego de Alcaraz.

Finally, Cabeza de Vaca and his companions were reunited with the countrymen for whom they had searched since leaving Florida more than seven years earlier.

Their joy, however, would not last long.■

Barely clothed, the four survivors of the Narváez Expedition, Cabeza de Vaca, Estebanico, Del Castillo, and Dorantes, set out on their journey as healers across Texas and into parts of the Southwest.

A QUIET HOMECOMING

Alcaraz and his men were on an expedition to capture Indian slaves. So Cabeza de Vaca's joy at finally finding other Spaniards soon turned to disappointment. They realized that their countrymen had not changed their attitudes toward the native people from whom they had been taking food, shelter, and land.

Alcaraz begged Cabeza de Vaca to send messengers to the Indians who were hiding in the woods to come forward and bring supplies. Cabeza de Vaca complied and over 600 Indians arrived with food still sealed in clay pots that had been buried for storage. The Spaniards accepted the food greedily and Cabeza de Vaca soon learned that they also planned to enslave these Indians. That led to bitter quarrels. The four former castaways may even have feared for their lives.

Rather than allow the Indians to be captured, Cabeza de Vaca and his men decided to leave the Spaniards and travel on. When the Indians got up to follow them, Alcaraz tried to persuade the Indians to stay. He told them that Cabeza de Vaca and his men were also Spaniards, and low-class Spaniards in addition. They shouldn't be trusted.

"The Indians gave all that talk of theirs little attention," Cabeza de Vaca wrote. "They parleyed among themselves, saying that the Christians lied, for we had come from sunrise, while the others came from where the sun sets; that we cured the sick while the others killed those who were healthy; that we went naked and shoeless, whereas the others wore clothes and went on horseback and with lances. Also, that we asked for nothing, but gave away all we were presented with, meanwhile the others seemed to have no other aim than to steal what they could, and never gave anything to anybody."

Cabeza de Vaca, however, was not interested in keeping disciples. He recognized the need for these people to return to their villages and plant crops and get on with their daily lives. After much discussion and persuasion, he finally convinced them to go home, though it must have been sad to part with people who had been with them for many months.

Cabeza de Vaca and his companions were turned over to a lieutenant who deliberately led them through a forest where they would not encounter other Indians. Cabeza de Vaca and his men later learned that as soon as they left the camp, Alcaraz and his men descended on the Indians who had been sent home and captured them.

The group continued traveling southwest in Mexico and approached the town of Culiacán. The *alcalde* (mayor) was Melchior Díaz, who had heard of Cabeza de Vaca and his travels. Díaz was one of the few Spaniards who genuinely wanted to help the Indians.

Again, Cabeza de Vaca was asked to summon the Indians out of hiding, but this time, Díaz did not intend to capture them. Rather, he believed that they should be converted to Christianity. When the Indians did arrive, Díaz told them that if they believed in God, the Spaniards would not mistreat them but if they did not, the Spaniards would take them as slaves. "They replied that they understood us thoroughly and would do as we had told," said Cabeza de Vaca.

This seemed to have a ripple effect throughout Mexico for as Cabeza de Vaca and Díaz set off for the village of San Miguel, they heard of Indian villages that had been repopulated, where churches were being built and crosses erected.

The four men rested a bit in San Miguel, then continued on to Compostela. When they arrived there in late May, the governor offered them clothing. But, as Cabeza de Vaca said, "I could not stand to wear any clothes for some time, or to sleep anywhere but on the bare floor."

Finally they arrived in Mexico City in July, 1536. They were welcomed as great heroes. They had journeyed nearly 6,000 miles since leaving Cuba.

Now it was time to go home.

Several attempts failed due to foul weather or damage to a ship. Finally, in April 1537, Cabeza de Vaca set sail from Veracruz, a port city on Mexico's east coast. After a brief stop at Havana, the ship took over a month to cross the Atlantic.

And it would have been too much to ask for a homecoming without one final problem.

As the ship passed the Azores, an island chain 1,000 miles off the coast of Portugal, it came within sight of a French pirate. The French were enemies of the Spanish. So the pirates pursued Cabeza de Vaca's ship and quickly caught up with it.

But after a decade of enduring harsh conditions, Cabeza de Vaca was finally due for a break. Rather than board the Spanish ship at night, the French captain decided to until wait until the next morning to seize his prey. The dawn revealed nine nearby Portuguese ships, which saved the Spanish vessel. The pirate ship escaped and Cabeza de Vaca's ship was escorted the rest of the way. They arrived in Lisbon, Portugal on August 9, 1537. It had been more than ten years since the day Cabeza de Vaca first set sail for the New World.

Many in Spain were well acquainted with the travels of Cabeza de Vaca and his companions, including Charles I, the king of Spain. He granted Cabeza de Vaca an audience in Seville. After a lengthy discussion, Cabeza de Vaca was assured that he would receive high honors and a new appointment for his service. That promise would not be immediately fulfilled.

The first offer he received was from Hernando de Soto, who had been appointed *adelantado* (governor) of Florida, just as Narváez and Ponce de León before him. He was also given the same mission, to conquer Florida for Spain. De Soto offered Cabeza de Vaca a position as second-in-command of the expedition back to Florida.

But Cabeza de Vaca passed up the offer. "He had had all he wanted of the swamps of Florida, and he had sworn to himself that he would never go on any expedition of which he did not have full control," wrote John Upton Terrell in his book *Journey into Darkness*.

He probably made a wise decision. In 1541, De Soto became the first European to cross the Mississippi River. But he suffered the same fate as Narváez, dying the following year as his expedition fell to pieces around him. In an interesting coincidence, the survivors constructed a fleet of small boats, sailed down the Mississippi and crossed the Gulf of Mexico to Pánuco—which had been Narváez' intended destination as well.

In the meantime, Cabeza de Vaca returned to his home in Jerez where by all accounts his wife still lived and had waited for him faithfully. She had also come into an inheritance that had allowed her to survive comfortably.

For her husband, the explorer, the transition back into civilized life was not an easy one. It's understandable that Cabeza de Vaca felt restless when he first returned to Jerez. Almost from the moment he landed, he was angling for a new commission in the New World.

Adding to the difficulty was his fame. "The curiosity of the people was insupportable. They constantly pestered him, asking his advice,

A modern day view of Asunción, Paraguay, this is the country's capital and the city where Cabeza de Vaca served as governor for four years from 1540–1544.

imploring (begging) him to find good posts for them in the Indies, begging for loans, imploring him to tell tales of his adventures, believing he had a hog's head of jewels secretly hidden in Seville," wrote Terrell.

In March 1540, more than two years after his return, Cabeza de Vaca finally received his promised appointment. The king designated him as the governor of the Province of Rio de la Plata in Paraguay. He sailed for South America eight months later.

Initially, Cabeza de Vaca flourished in his new position. He was able to communicate with the native Indians and end unrest. He even explored areas of the jungle that had never been seen by white men. True to his vow of tolerance toward native people, Cabeza de Vaca did not allow mistreatment of the natives.

But he was unsuccessful in his efforts to protect them. The lust for riches by his countrymen would hurt him in the end.

His own men turned against him and brought false charges against him. In April 1544, he was arrested and thrown into prison. The following year, like Christopher Columbus, he was taken in chains back to Spain. Early in 1546, his enemies struck. He was brought before the Royal Council of the Indies in Madrid, Spain's capital. He was accused of robbery and other crimes during his time in Paraguay. He was even accused of mistreating the Indians. Many people spoke out against him. He hoped that witnesses who would support his side of the story would return from Paraguay. But very few of them did, and after a long trial he was found guilty in 1551. He was banned from ever returning to the Americas.

The ordeal left him broken in spirit and health. Just as important, he was dishonored. And he was virtually penniless.

He spent his last years in an effort to clear his name. He also published a second edition of *La Relación* in 1555. It included descriptions of his time in Paraguay.

To help make his life a little easier, King Charles authorized an annual pension payment to him in 1556. But it was too little, too late.

Most historians believe that he died later that year or sometime in 1557. No one knows where he is buried.■

After hearing of the adventures of Cabeza de Vaca, Francisco Vásquez de Coronado returned to the Southwest United States in 1540, hoping to claim more gold and land for Spain.

THE LEGACY

At the end of his life, Álvar Núñez Cabeza de Vaca was probably not sure how he would be remembered. He was born at a time when the world was changing so quickly that many changes took place in a violent manner. As the Spaniards began to explore new worlds, they truly believed that they were far superior to any new people that they encountered.

Cabeza de Vaca was no different when he began his first great expedition but he would be completely changed by his experiences. His view of native people as individuals, and not savages, would be one of his most important legacies.

From *La Relación*, we know about Native American tribes who were probably gone before settlers arrived later. His description of each tribe painted a portrait of their behavior never before witnessed. "Recounting this period in his incomparable saga, Cabeza de Vaca sets down the first known accounts of the aborigines (natives) who inhabited the Texas coastal area and the adjacent territory," confirmed Terrell.

There were the Attácapas and the Karankawas who they encountered on the Island of Ill Fortune. Cabeza de Vaca spent a year with the Cahoques and was assisted in his effort to become a trader thanks to the friendly Charrucos located in Texas. He witnessed tribal wars between the Doguenes, who held him as a slave, and the Quevenes. The Mariames would be the final masters of Cabeza de Vaca and Andrés Dorantes, while the Iguaces were the final masters of Castillo and Estebanico. The Mariames and Iguaces were later identified as members of the Tónkawa Indians. After they escaped and traveled freely as medicine men, they were hosted by many tribes including the Arbadaos, Cuchendados, and the Pintos or Blancos.

Like anthropologists today who journey to remote parts of the world to live with the few remaining native tribes on earth, Cabeza de Vaca and his companions lived with these tribes, first as slaves and later as healers. Some had customs that may seem barbaric. The Mariames, for example, discarded girl babies because they did not want their daughters to marry into other tribes and have their children. Females were bought from their enemies to serve as wives.

The natives Cabeza de Vaca encountered also had admirable habits. For example, they shared food and supplies and lived communally with each other. Most importantly, they appeared willing to accept people of other cultures so long as they exhibited diplomacy rather than violence.

Another important legacy is that his journey revealed the true size of the North American continent. According to Hallenbeck, "Prior to his remarkable overland journey, Europe believed this continent to be quite narrow. Even the Spanish, who at this time knew more of America than all other nations combined, had the idea that the continent northward from lower Mexico was of about the same width and latitude of Mexico City."

Hallenbeck adds that Cabeza de Vaca's journey also sparked interest in Spain to explore the land north of Mexico. The famous expedition of Francisco Vásquez de Coronado between 1540 and 1542, which went through Arizona, New Mexico and Texas and reached as far as Kansas, came about as a direct result of Cabeza's visit to Mexico City. Later, Francisco de Ibarra explored northern Mexico in what is now the state of Chihuahua.

Cabeza de Vaca learned to appreciate the cultures he observed, rather than destroy them. That made him unique among the Spanish adventurers of his era.

"He never questioned the right of Europeans to rule the New World," wrote Michael Wood in *Conquistadors*. "What he wanted was for that rule to be benevolent (for the good of the people being ruled)."

And his personal account of his adventure is not only one of the most important historical documents of the time but also a testament to his character as well.

The famous naval historian Samuel Eliot Morison wrote one of the best summaries: "Álvar Núñez Cabeza de Vaca stands out as a truly noble and humane character. Nowhere in the lurid history of the Conquest does one find such integrity and devotion to Christian principles in the face of envy, malice, treachery, cruelty, lechery, and plain greed." ■

CHRONOLOGY

1490	born in Jerez de la Frontera, Spain
1511	receives first military assignment in war between France and Italy
1520	is appointed to command a city gate outside of Seville, the Puerta del Ossario; also may have married around this time
1527	is made treasurer of the expedition to conquer Florida led by Pánfilo Narváez
1528	lands in Florida; eventually cast ashore on the Island of Ill Fortune
1529-1530	lives as a slave with the Karankawas of the Island of Ill Fortune
1530-1533	becomes a trader of goods to the Indians
1533	returns to being a slave after encountering fellow Spaniards Alonso del Castillo, Andrés Dorantes, and the black slave Estebanico
1534	escapes from the Mariames Indians with del Castillo, Dorantes, and Estebanico; begin their journey as medicine men

1536	encounters Spaniards after traveling across Texas to the west coast of Mexico
1537	returns to Spain
1540	is appointed governor of the Province of Rio de la Plata, Paraguay; arrives in Paraguay
1542	publishes *La Relación*, the account of his journeys in the New World
1544	is arrested and jailed in Paraguay
1545	returns in chains to Spain
1546	placed on trial in Spain, accused of numerous crimes while in Paraguay
1551	is convicted of crimes and barred from returning to the New World
1555	publishes second edition of *La Relación*, which includes his stay in Paraguay
1556/7?	dies

TIMELINE IN HISTORY

1492 Christopher Columbus discovers New World

1498 Vasco da Gama discovers sea route to India by sailing around the southern tip of Africa

1500 Juan de la Cosa publishes the first map of the New World

1502 Montezuma II becomes emperor of Aztec nation in Mexico

1513 Vasco Núñez de Balboa crosses Isthmus of Panama and discovers Pacific Ocean; Juan Ponce de León discovers Florida

1519 Hernán Cortés enters the Aztec capital city Tenochtitlan and is received by Montezuma II, the Aztec ruler

1521 Cortés assumes control of Mexico for Spain

1526 Esteban Gomez establishes but soon abandons settlement on the Savannah River (present-day Georgia)

1527 Álvar Núñez Cabeza de Vaca begins ill-fated expedition to Florida

1531 Francisco Pizarro begins conquest of Peru

1534 Jacques Cartier begins exploring the St. Lawrence River for France

1538 geographer Gerardus Mercator uses "America" to refer to the entire New World for the first time

1540 Francisco Vásquez de Coronado sets off on expedition from Mexico that eventually passes through Arizona, New Mexico, Texas, Oklahoma and Kansas

1541 Hernando de Soto discovers Mississippi River

1542 Juan Rodriguez Cabrillo and Bartolome Ferrelo explore west coast of North America as far north of Oregon

1551 Real y Pontificia Universidad de Mexico becomes first university on the North American continent

1555 tobacco brought from America to Spain for the first time

1565 Pedro Menéndez de Avilés establishes St. Augustine, Florida, which becomes oldest U.S. city.

1607 Jamestown colony founded

FOR FURTHER READING

Arrington, Carolyn. *Estevanico, Black Explorer in Spanish Texas*. Austin, TX: Eakin Press, 1986.

Baker, Betty. *Walk the World's Rim*. New York: HarperCollins Children's Books, 1965.

Brandt, Keith. *Cabeza de Vaca: New World Explorer*. Mahwah, NJ: Troll Associates, 1993.

Johnston, Lissa Jones. *Crossing a Continent: The Incredible Story of Cabeza de Vaca*. Austin, TX: Eakin Publications, 2002.

Long, Haniel. *The Marvelous Adventure of Cabeza de Vaca*. Santa Fe, NM: Bear & Co., 1992

Wade, Mary Dodson. *Cabeza de Vaca: Conquistador Who Cared*. New York: Colophon Books, 1994.

ON THE WEB

Windows to the Unknown: Cabeza de Vaca's Journey to the Southwest
http://www.english.swt.edu/css/vacaindex.HTML

PBS - Alvar Núñez Cabeza de Vaca
http://www.pbs.org/weta/thewest/people/a_c/cabezadevaca.htm

The Handbook of Texas Online: Cabeza de Vaca, Alvar Nuñez
http://www.tsha.utexas.edu/handbook/online/articles/view/CC/fca6.html

The Narvaez/Vaca Expedition
http://sites.gulf.net/pal/narvaezvaca.html

Cabeza de Vaca (complete translation of *La Relación*)
http://ojinaga.com/cabeza/

GLOSSARY

ardor (AR-der): strong enthusiasm

ambushed (AM-bushed): attacked by surprise

barbaric (bar-BEAR-ik): savage, uncivilized

barge (barj): flat boat used for carrying freight, usually pulled by another boat

brutality (broo-TAL-ih-tee): cruelty or harshness

cargo (KAR-go): a load or freight which is carried, usually by a ship or an aircraft

capsized (KAP-syzd): overturned

caulking (KAWK-ing): material used to seal cracks or seams to make airtight or watertight

commission (kuh-MISH-un): the authority to carry out a certain task or duty

communally (kuh-MYOO-nuhl-ee): equally by the people of a community

compelled (kuhm-PEHLD): forced

complied (kuhm-PLYD): agreed to; acted in accordance with the wishes of another

conquistadors (cahn-KEES-tuh-dawr-ays): Spanish explorers who conquered vast territories in the New World

conservative (kuhn-SUR-vuh-tiv): traditional or moderate

converted (kuhn-VURT-id): changed

countered (KOWN-turd): opposed, answered

diplomatic (dip-luh-MAT-ik): fair

edible (ED-uh-buhl): suitable to be eaten

endure (en-DOOR): survive despite hardships

enlightened (en-LYT-end): educated

enslave (en-SLAYV): capture

flourished (FLUR-ishd): grew, thrived

fortify (FOR-tuh-fy): strengthen

gauge (gayj): measure

heretic (HAIR-ih-tik): someone who questions religious faith

inarticulate (in-ar-TIK-you-lit): not good with words

incredible (in-KRED-uh-buhl): unbelievable

indigenous (in-DIJ-uh-nus): native, original

infidel (IN-fi-del): heretic, atheist

inland (IN-lind): upriver, away from a body of water

inquisitive (in-QWIZ-ih-tiv): curious

insupportable (in-suh-PORT-uh-buhl): unbearable

lowly (LO-lee): humble

merciless (MUR-sih-lis): cruel

Moors: race composed of Arabs and Berbers who conquered and inhabited Spain between the eighth and fifteenth centuries

notary (NO-tuh-ree): legal representative

notorious (no-TOR-ee-uhs): famous, usually unfavorably

parlayed: increased in value, traded up

peninsula (puh-NIN-suh-luh): a land mass surrounded on three sides by water

plight (plyt): trouble

provincial (pruh-VIN-shul): unsophisticated

Renaissance (REN-ih-sans): transitional period in Europe between 14th and 17th centuries, marked by growth of arts, literature, and science

repopulate (re-POP-yuh-layt): breed, to return inhabitants to a certain area

reserves (re-ZURVS): savings, capital

resin (REZ-in): gum, tree sap

resourceful (ree-SORS-fuhl): using creativity in difficult situations

romanticized (ro-MAN-tih-syzd): idealized

ruthless (ROOTH-lis): brutal

scorn (skorn): express contempt toward

sporadically (spuh-RAD-ik-lee): now and then, irregularly

spurred: encouraged

thunderstruck (THUN-duhr-struk): shocked

thwarted: stopped, prevented

vying: competing

INDEX